History *of* Britain
Life on a
Victorian
Steamship

Andrew Langley

Illustrated by Gerald Wood

HISTORY OF BRITAIN – LIFE ON A VICTORIAN STEAMSHIP
was produced for Heinemann Children's Reference
by Lionheart Books, London.

Editors: Lionel Bender, Sue Reid
Designer: Ben White
Editorial Assistant: Madeleine Samuel
Picture Researcher: Jennie Karrach
Media Conversion and Typesetting: Peter MacDonald

Educational Consultant: Jane Shuter
Editorial Advisors: Andrew Farrow, Paul Shuter

Production Controller: Lorraine Stebbing
Editorial Director: David Riley

First published in Great Britain in 1997 by
Heinemann Educational Publishers, a division of Reed
Educational and Professional Publishing Limited,
Halley Court, Jordan Hill, Oxford OX2 8EJ.

MADRID ATHENS
FLORENCE PRAGUE WARSAW
PORTSMOUTH NH CHICAGO SAO PAULO MEXICO
SINGAPORE TOKYO MELBOURNE AUCKLAND
IBADAN GABORONE JOHANNESBURG KAMPALA NAIROBI

© Reed Educational & Professional Publishing Ltd 1997

ISBN 0 431 057117 Hb   ISBN 0 431 05715XPb

British Library Cataloguing-in-Publication Data.
A catalogue record for this book is available
from the British Library.

Printed in Italy

Acknowledgements
Picture credits
t = top, b = bottom, l = left, r = right, c = centre.
Pages 4tr: John Frost Historical Newspapers/*The Times*. 4c: Mary Evans
Picture Library/*Illustrated London News*. 4b, 5, 6-7, 8c, 8r, 9: National
Maritime Museum, London. 8l: The Royal Collection © Her Majesty The
Queen. 10t, 10b: National Maritime Museum, London. 10c: Science &
Society Picture Library. 12, 13t: National Maritime Museum, London.
13cr: E. Greig Collection/The Ephemera Society. 14:The Bridgeman Art
Library/Birmingham City Museums & Art Gallery. 15: Public Record Office.
16, 17t, 17c: National Maritime Museum, London. 17b: Mary Evans Picture
Library. 18b: e. t. archive/The Tate Gallery. 18c: National Maritime
Museum. 19: Trustees of the Tate Gallery. 20t, 21b: National Maritime
Museum, London. 20b: The University of Liverpool Library. 21t: E. Greig
Collection/The Ephemera Society.

All artwork by Gerald Wood except map on page 23 by Stephan
Chabluk.
Cover: Artwork by Gerald Wood.

PLACES TO VISIT

Here are some museums and steam and sailing ships
preserved from the Victorian era. Your local tourist office will
be able to tell you about places to visit in your area.

Cutty Sark, Greenwich, London. This beautiful sailing clipper
was one of the last challengers to the supremacy of steam
during the 19th century.

Dock Museum, Barrow-in-Furness, Cumbria. See how some
of the earliest steel ships were built in this Victorian dock.

The *Flying Buzzard*, Maryport, Cumbria. A preserved steam
tugboat, built on the River Clyde.

Hartlepool Historic Ships, Northumbria. Exhibits include the
paddle steamer *Wingfield Castle*.

Historic Dockyard, Chatham, Kent. The site where Royal
Naval ships were built for nearly 400 years.

Maritime and Industrial Museum, Swansea, West
Glamorgan. Display of local marine history set in the old
warehouses and docks.

Maritime Museum, Exeter, Devon. A varied collection of
over 100 historic craft.

Merseyside Maritime Museum, Liverpool. Exhibits at one of
the major ports of Victorian times.

National Maritime Museum, Greenwich, London. Huge
variety of exhibits on the history of British seagoing.

Paddle Steamer *Waverley*, Glasgow. The world's last seagoing paddle steamer, still running excursions.

Portsmouth Historic Ships, Portsmouth, Hampshire. Among
the exhibits is HMS *Warrior*, Britain's first iron-clad warship.

Scottish Maritime Museum, Irvine, Ayrshire. Climb aboard
many historic ships, including a steam-powered cargo boat.

SS *Great Britain*, Bristol, Avon. Isambard Kingdom Brunel's
great iron ship, now being restored to her original glory.

SS *Shieldhall*, Southampton, Hampshire. The largest
preserved working steamship in Britain, in the process of
being renovated.

Steam Yacht *Gondola*, Coniston Water, Cumbria. Built in
1859, this beautiful steam yacht still carries sightseers
round Lake Coniston.

Windermere Steamboat Museum, Cumbria. Collection of
small, powered boats, including a steamer built in 1850.

INTRODUCTION

In June 1819, the ship *Savannah* reached Liverpool from New York. It had sailed most of the way, but was helped by paddle wheels, turned by a steam engine. This was the first time a steam-powered boat had crossed the Atlantic. By 1838, vessels were making the whole crossing using steam power, and in only 15 days. A sailing ship might take 40 days!

During Queen Victoria's reign (1837-1901), steam slowly took over from sail. Steamships were faster and did not have to wait for winds and tides. Gradually, screw propellers replaced the clumsy paddles and big ships were built of iron instead of wood. More and more people made the journeys from Britain to the United States of America (USA), India and Australia.

CONTENTS

AT THE DOCKS

In 1835, the engineer Isambard Kingdom Brunel planned a railway from London to Bristol. Someone said the line was very long. "Why not make it longer", replied Brunel, "and have a steamboat go from Bristol to New York?"

▷ **Adverts in an 1852 newspaper** (above right). The steamship owners are looking for passengers who want to travel from Liverpool, Glasgow, Southampton or London to the USA.

▷ **Irish emigrants are blessed by their priest** before beginning the long sea journey to the USA.

By 1838, Brunel had built the *Great Western*. It was one of the first of many steamships to carry passengers regularly across the Atlantic. Steamships competed for business with hundreds of passenger sailing ships, or 'packets'. In 1837, when Victoria became queen, more than 80,000 people left Britain to settle in other countries. Most went to the USA, but others sailed to parts of the British Empire, such as Canada, South Africa and Australia. By 1849, the figure had shot up to 300,000.

▷ **Waiting for the ship – from Alfred Withers' diary.** He and his wife travelled from Liverpool to Melbourne in 1857 in the *James Baines*. It was their honeymoon. Withers kept a record of the 80- day voyage, with his own illustrations. At this time, more than 20,000 Britons were emigrating to Australia each year.

Great Western Steamship Line.
BRISTOL AND NEW YORK.

SOMERSET	..	2000 Tons	..	WM. WESTERN, Commander.
CORNWALL	..	2000	..	WM. STAMPER, ,,
GREAT WESTERN	..	2000	..	S. WINDHAM, ,,
ARRAGON	..	1300	..	GEORGE SYMONS, ,,

The Vessels of this Line carry only a limited number of Passengers, every attention being paid to their comfort and convenience.

RATES OF PASSAGE.

SALOON.—Thirteen Guineas for each Adult; Children under twelve years, 21s. per year; Infants, One Guinea. Return Tickets available for twelve calendar months from date of issue. Twenty Guineas.

These Rates include a liberal Table, without Wines or Liquors, which can be obtained on board.

£5 deposit is required to secure Saloon Berths, the balance to be paid before sailing. No charge for Steward's Fee.

SECOND CABIN Passage to New York, Boston, or Philadelphia, Eight Guineas; Children under eight, half fare; Infants under twelve months, One Guinea.

Second Cabin Passengers are provided with Beds, Bedding, and all necessary Utensils. Wash

◁ **A poster listing the ships and fares for Brunel's steamship company.** The vessels took goods and passengers, who paid up to 20 guineas (£21) for a return ticket from Bristol to New York. The fares included meals, bedding, and insurance for delays, loss of goods and risks from fires.

Why did so many people want to travel abroad? Most were poor or jobless emigrants who hoped to find better work and wages in a new land. Many Scots and Irish were forced from their homes by greedy landlords or hunger. A million Irish people emigrated to the USA in the late 1840s after a terrible famine. Some dreamed of great riches. When gold was discovered in California in 1849, thousands of Britons crossed the Atlantic to try and make their fortunes. The emigrants were crammed together in the 'steerage', a large space below the ship's deck. Richer passengers could afford a private cabin.

◁ **Passengers line the quayside of a busy port**, waiting to board a paddle steamer that will take them to the USA. Meanwhile, cargo and mail is loaded into other ships. Steamers were faster and more likely to be on time than sailing ships. So they were used to carry the Royal Mail overseas.

INSIDE THE STEAMSHIP

Early steamships were built of wood, just like sailing ships. They had masts and rigging for the sails, which assisted the steam engines. The engines used so much coal that often some of it had to be stacked on the deck as well as stored in the hold.

The ships were pushed along by huge paddle wheels fitted on each side. But these did not work well. Screw propellers were much more efficient. Brunel's *Great Britain*, built in 1843, was the first big ship to be fitted with one. It was also the first big ship to be built of iron. Iron vessels did not leak, like wooden ones, and were much stronger.

▽ **The ship has a large flat deck with wooden 'houses' built on top.** Some of these deckhouses were used as cabins for the first-class passengers.

△ **Workers building the *Great Eastern*,** Brunel's third huge steamship, in 1858. She was six times bigger than any other ship.

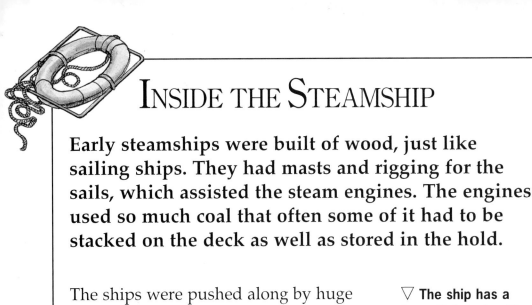

▷ **Cutaway view of an iron-hulled steamship of the early 1850s,** carrying emigrants across the Atlantic. It has room for 52 first-class passengers, 85 second-class, and 400 steerage class passengers.

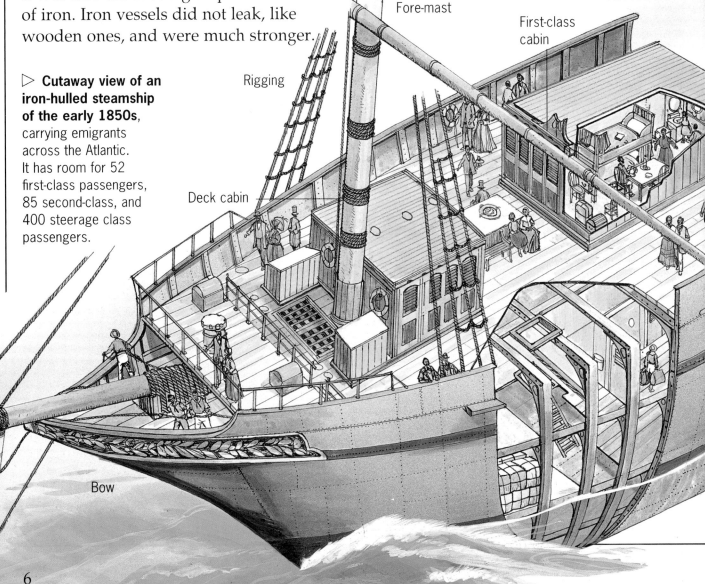

Fore-mast

Starboard

First-class cabin

Rigging

Deck cabin

First-class cabin

Bow

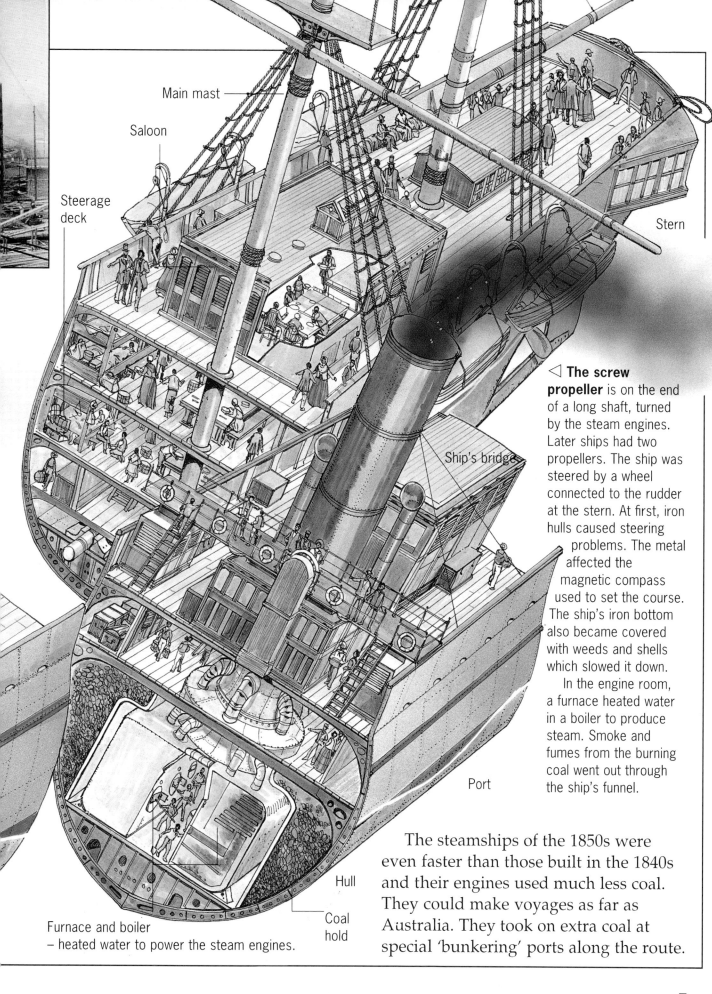

Main mast

Saloon

Steerage deck

Stern

Ship's bridge

◁ **The screw propeller** is on the end of a long shaft, turned by the steam engines. Later ships had two propellers. The ship was steered by a wheel connected to the rudder at the stern. At first, iron hulls caused steering problems. The metal affected the magnetic compass used to set the course. The ship's iron bottom also became covered with weeds and shells which slowed it down.

In the engine room, a furnace heated water in a boiler to produce steam. Smoke and fumes from the burning coal went out through the ship's funnel.

Port

Hull

Coal hold

Furnace and boiler – heated water to power the steam engines.

The steamships of the 1850s were even faster than those built in the 1840s and their engines used much less coal. They could make voyages as far as Australia. They took on extra coal at special 'bunkering' ports along the route.

7

CAPTAIN AND CREW

The captain had to make sure that ship, cargo and people on board completed the voyage safely. So he had to be obeyed – not just by his crew, but by the passengers as well. "What he says and does is law for all alike", wrote one traveller in the 1880s.

The captain was helped by his officers (sometimes known as 'mates'), who each took one of the four-hour 'watches' (periods of duty) on the bridge every day. Each officer also had his own special job to do. The chief officer was the second-in-command. He ran the ship when the captain was asleep or if he was ill. He was also in charge of the seamen, the masts and rigging and the navigating (steering) of the ship.

Next in command was the second officer, who looked after the loading and unloading of the cargo in port. Then came the third officer, who dealt with the mails, and the fourth officer, who took care of the baggage.

△ **Albert Edward, Prince of Wales, in a sailor suit** in 1848. At the time, sailors had only just begun to wear a regular uniform.

△ **Deck of the Ceylon,** a steamship built in 1858.

▷ **An officer's sea chest** from the Peninsular and Oriental Steam Navigation Company.

△ **A seaman and a ship's boy.** (Boys as young as 14 went to sea as apprentices.) They are in new uniforms, issued by the company that owns the ship. Before about 1860, seamen usually had to make their own clothes out of old canvas sails. To keep out the wet, they coated the canvas with tar.

△ **The commander or captain** (third from right) of the *Great Eastern*, with his officers. Once the voyage had begun, the captain was in full control. Before the invention of radio in 1901, there was no link with the shore so he had to make all decisions himself.

The captain had an enormous amount of duties to worry about. He had to navigate the ship, and keep control of his officers and crew. He made sure that the passengers were happy and well-behaved and he took the religious service which was held each Sunday. He invited cabin passengers to dine at his table.

△ **Stokers and other crew members.** Large ships needed as many as 60 stokers to tend the ship's furnaces. Steamships also needed a huge variety of skilled men. Cooks, butchers and bakers prepared the food. Carpenters, blacksmiths, rope- and sail-makers kept the ship in good repair.

△ **Junior officers.** On smart shipping lines, officers wore uniforms like those of the Royal Navy. Senior officers had different numbers of brass buttons and gold stripes on their frock-coats to show their superior rank, but junior officers had no marks at all. Crew members wore their smartest uniforms when going into port.

For the passengers, the most important officer was the purser. He supplied them with food and drink and solved their problems over cabin bedding, furniture and other equipment. The purser also paid the crew their wages.

A steamship needed a new kind of officer. This was the chief engineer, who was in charge of the engines and the team of mechanics, stokers, boilermen and firemen who operated them.

Below the officers was the boatswain (pronounced 'bosun'). He made sure that the crew carried out the officers' orders. He was helped by three or four bosun's 'mates'. At the bottom of the line of command came the seamen. They did the hard work – tying up the ship in port, handling cargo, raising the anchor, setting the sails, making repairs and cleaning the decks. A steamship needed at least 40 seamen and stokers.

LIFE AT SEA

A seaman was often in danger. On early steamships he still had to climb the masts to alter sails. An emigrant described how one sailor "fell from the yard-arm (sail pole). With a heavy sea rolling ... nothing could possibly be done to save him."

△ **A ship's bell.** It was rung to mark the 'watches'.

There were perils on deck, too. The seaman's greatest fear was fire, and this could easily start in a wooden steamship. Sparks flew from the funnel. Pipes and pistons became scorching hot. Blazing coals fell out of the furnaces.

Deadly diseases such as typhus spread quickly in a crowded passenger ship. In some parts of the world, such as the China Seas, there were still pirates who attacked merchant ships. But the greatest danger of all was shipwreck. Even iron ships might be holed by icebergs or smashed on rocks. During the 1860s, over 2,000 British seaman lost their lives each year while working on ship.

▽ **The Great Western,** a wooden paddle steamship, battles through a giant wave during a hurricane on her fifth crossing to New York in 1838. Wooden vessels were in danger of breaking up in heavy seas.

▷ **The Great Britain lies stranded on the beach** in Dundrum Bay in County Down, Ireland, in September 1846. The ship was on a voyage to New York, but on a dark wet night the captain mistook a lighthouse and took the wrong course. The passengers had to be lowered over the sides and put on other ships. The Great Britain could not be re-floated until the following year. It was then towed to Liverpool to be repaired.

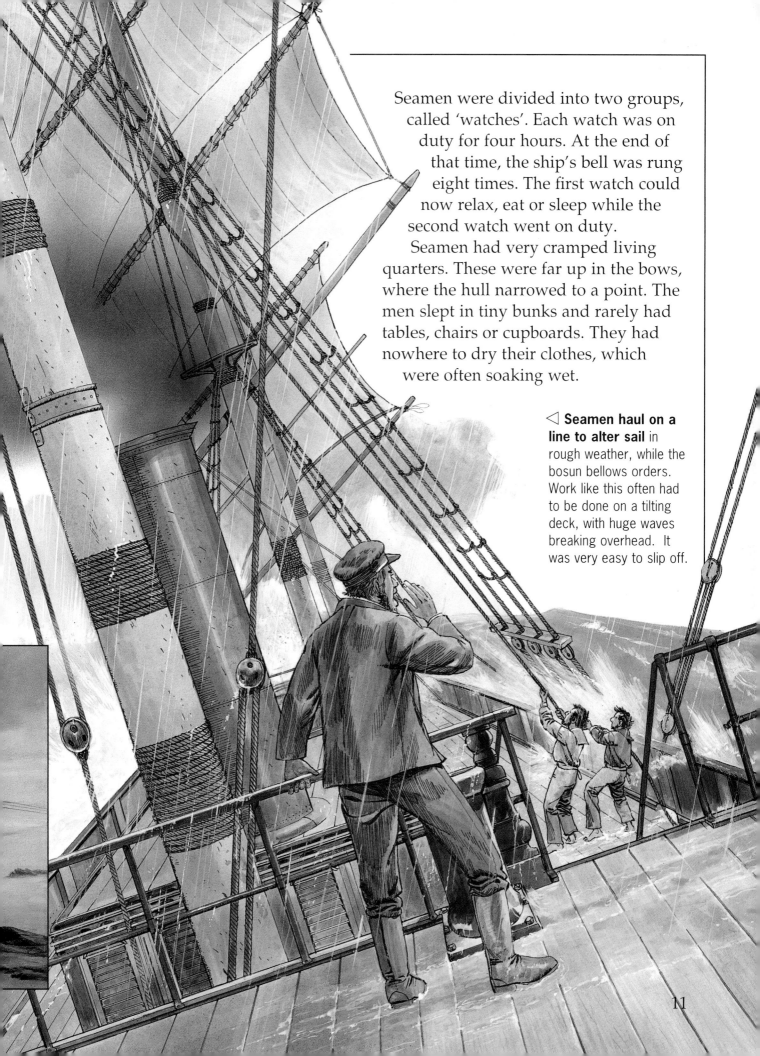

Seamen were divided into two groups, called 'watches'. Each watch was on duty for four hours. At the end of that time, the ship's bell was rung eight times. The first watch could now relax, eat or sleep while the second watch went on duty.

Seamen had very cramped living quarters. These were far up in the bows, where the hull narrowed to a point. The men slept in tiny bunks and rarely had tables, chairs or cupboards. They had nowhere to dry their clothes, which were often soaking wet.

◁ **Seamen haul on a line to alter sail** in rough weather, while the bosun bellows orders. Work like this often had to be done on a tilting deck, with huge waves breaking overhead. It was very easy to slip off.

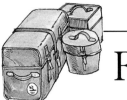

FIRST-CLASS

Only rich people could afford the £30 or £40 (£3,000-£4,000 in today's money) for a first-class passage to the USA. For this they got a tiny cabin, shared with up to three others. They could also use the first-class saloon and a specially reserved area of the deck.

The first-class cabin was often less than 3 metres square, with bunk beds against one side. The only place to sit was a hard sofa or chair. There were hooks for clothes, a small mirror and two washbasins. Private lavatories were rare. Most passengers had to make do with a china pot emptied through the porthole.

The cabins were often dark. Portholes and skylights let in little light, so cabins were lit by candles or oil lamps. These were put out at night because of the risk of fire.

▽ **A second-class cabin on board the** *Saxonia* (below). First-class cabins were just as cramped (right). This lady is trying to dress, helped by her maid. But, as the ship lurches, boxes and brushes slide to the floor and furniture topples over.

△ **An engineer**, going to Canada by steamship to oversee the building of a railway. British engineers were in great demand, because they were the first to develop railways, steam engines and giant bridges. Among them was Robert Stephenson, who built the Victoria Bridge in Canada in 1859. With faster voyages, many people travelled to the USA on business. The writer Charles Dickens made a reading tour of the USA in 1842.

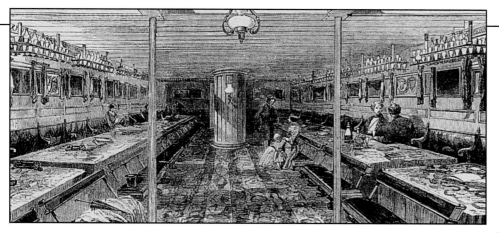

◁ **The grand saloon** for cabin passengers on the steamship *Great Britain*. There was a carpet on the floor.

▽ **Steamship baggage label** for the Cunard Line.

TO BE LANDED AT **NEW YORK**

1st CUNARD LINE SALOON BAGGAGE FOR

Name _____
Per S.S. _____
Date of Sailing _____
From (port) _____
Final Destination _____

DECK _____
STATE ROOM Nº _____

WANTED ON THE **VOYAGE**

TO BE LANDED AT **NEW YORK**

The saloon was much bigger, being up to 15 metres long. On early steamships, saloons had just a table down the middle with benches on either side. Glasses and bottles were kept on a long shelf above. The best saloons were set in the stern of the ship, where large windows gave fine views. On Atlantic crossings, passengers were glad of the heat from a fireplace or stove.

△ **This family of emigrants** is rich enough to travel first-class. The three children and their nursemaid have a separate cabin. Not everyone who emigrated was poor or jobless. Many were members of the professional classes. Lawyers, doctors, teachers and factory owners saw that there were opportunities to become successful in the new and fast-growing American cities. Many women travelled to the USA to find rich husbands.

△ **A wealthy couple on their way to visit the USA.** They were among the first 'tourists', who travelled for pleasure. Sportsmen also went to the USA to hunt wild animals. Other tourists went east to see the ruins of ancient Egypt.

In Steerage

Directly below the first-class cabins were the emigrants. They lived in the cramped area called the steerage. "It was horrid to be herded together like beasts", wrote one emigrant in the 1880s.

They had little room to move around. The area was lined with rows of double bunks. Parents took the top bunk, and their children the one below. In this space, each family had to eat, sleep and store their belongings. A long, wide table ran down the centre.

In this way, some emigrant ships could pack in as many as 700 people. There was no chance of any privacy. People often had to share a bunk with a total stranger. Then in the 1840s new laws forced shipowners to give single men and women separate quarters (living areas). The women lived in the stern, the married couples in the middle and the single men at the bow.

▷ (Above right) **Family quarters in the steerage.** In the foreground, parents sort through baggage for fresh clothes for their baby. In the background, a boy and his mother prepare food for his sick father who is resting in a bunk. An open hatchway lets in light now, but in bad weather it would be tightly covered over. Seawater dribbles down the mast from waves which wash over the deck. Damp was yet another discomfort for steerage passengers.

◁ **The Last of England** – a Victorian painting showing two newly wed emigrants sheltering from the wind and sea spray on deck a steamship to the USA. They were hoping for a better life in another country. In the background is a lifeboat.

△ **This family has travelled from Ireland**, which was then a very poor country. About half of Irish people lived on small farms. Their main source of food was potatoes. In 1845 and 1846, disease ruined the Irish potato crop. This caused a dreadful famine in which over one million people died during the next five years. Two million more joined a rush to emigrate to the USA between 1847 and 1861.

△ **A family of Scottish emigrants.** Like many thousands of other landworkers, they have been forced from their home in the Highlands by English landlords. The landlords' actions created much bitterness in the Highlands. Villages were knocked down to make room for more valuable flocks of sheep to graze. Homeless, the family walked to Glasgow to buy their steerage ticket to the USA. This cost £4 (£400 in today's money).

△ **A brother and sister from Manchester.** He was thrown out of work when a factory closed, and she sewed clothes for which she was paid very little money. They are going to join the flood of settlers moving westwards on to the vast American prairies.

▽ **A health warning** to emigrants about a disease on-board ships.

CHOLERA having made its appearance on board several Passenger Ships proceeding from the United Kingdom to the United States of America, and having, in some instances, been very fatal, Her Majesty's Colonial Land and Emigration Commissioners feel it their duty to recommend to the Parents of Families in which there are many young children, and to all persons in weak health who may be contemplating Emigration, to postpone their departure until a milder season. There can be no doubt that the sea sickness consequent on the rough weather which Ships must encounter at this season, joined to the cold and damp of a sea voyage, will render persons who are not strong more susceptible to the attacks of this disease.

To those who may Emigrate at this season the Commissioners strongly recommend that they should provide themselves with as much warm clothing as they can, and especially with flannel, to be worn next the Skin; that they should have both their clothes and their persons quite clean before embarking, and should be careful to keep them so during the voyage,—and that they should provide themselves with as much solid and wholesome food as they can procure, in addition to the Ship's allowance to be used on the voyage. It would, of course, be desirable, if they can arrange it, that they should not go in a Ship that is much crowded, or that is not provided with a Medical Man.

By Order of the Board,

S. WALCOTT,
Secretary.

Colonial Land and Emigration Office,
9, Park Street, Westminster,
November, 1853.

The steerage was also very dim. There were a few oil lamps, and the only other light came through tiny portholes. The low ceiling, just high enough for an adult to stand up in, made it seem even gloomier.

In bad weather, the portholes and the hatch above were closed to stop seawater flooding in. Unable to go on deck, the emigrants were imprisoned in virtual darkness. If the storm lasted several days, the stench of vomit, stale food and sweat became disgusting. It is no surprise that diseases such as dysentery spread quickly among people in the steerage.

EATING AND DRINKING

"We have a regular farmyard on board", wrote a steamship passenger in 1858. There were no refrigerators, so ships carried plenty of fresh food. This included hens (for eggs), cattle, sheep and goats (for milk and meat). They were usually kept on deck.

▽ **The deck of the steamship *Ceylon*.** Sides of freshly killed meat hang on the right. Vegetables were often grown in the lifeboats.

◁ **The ship's galley (kitchen).** The cooks prepare the dishes, which a waiter carries through to passengers in the first-class saloon beyond.

◁ **After dinner, cabin passengers** often strolled on deck, as here on the *Great Eastern*.

▽ **The first-class passengers dine in the grand saloon of the *Ormuz*.** They sat in swivel chairs. The bases of the chairs were bolted to the deck to stop them moving in rough seas.

Life on a long voyage could be very dull. Cabin passengers looked forward to mealtimes as exciting parts of the day. There was plenty of food – and it was free! Dinner was the biggest and grandest meal, and included several kinds of fresh meat, as well as fish bought from passing fishing boats. The P & O Line even provided first-class passengers with as much free beer, wine and spirits as they liked.

Down in steerage, eating was much less grand. On early steamships, emigrants usually brought their own food. They had to queue to have the food cooked in the ship's galley. During the 1850s, William Inman became the first shipowner to provide good food free for his steerage passengers.

Several things could spoil a meal, whatever class you were travelling in. Heavy waves might put out the galley fire so that nothing could be cooked. A sudden lurch of the ship might make diners slide from their seats. And those who were seasick, of course, would not eat at all.

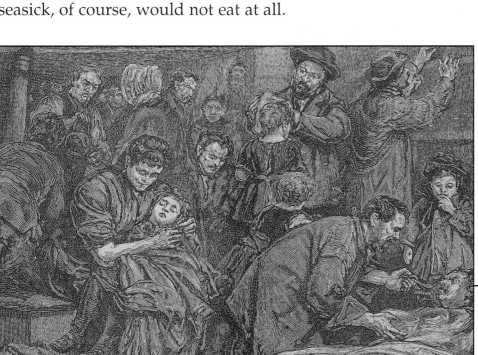

◁ **In the steerage,** passengers would often have to eat where they rested and slept – in a space 2 metres square shared with other people for the whole voyage. In some ships, a ration of food was served out to each family once a week. By the end of the voyage, these rations had often gone rotten.

PASSING THE TIME

Steamships took at least two weeks to reach the USA, and six weeks to reach Australia. In bad weather, passengers usually stayed below decks. In fine weather, they could walk in the open air.

How did they amuse themselves? Some emigrants used the time to learn to read and write. Some went to the daily religious services. Many read books, or wrote diaries of the voyage. Others played cards, or board games such as chess. Later, luxury ships had billiard tables which were hung so that they stayed level whatever the weather.

There were also noisier pastimes. Most saloons had a piano and concerts would be arranged to entertain cabin passengers. There were dances and fancy-dress parties. Steerage travellers danced and sang to the music of concertinas and fiddles.

But most time was spent in sitting, talking and swapping stories. In this way, many emigrants became friends.

▷ **Steerage passengers enjoy themselves on the fore deck.** Some in the bow watch a school of porpoises playing in the water. The steamer is about to overtake a sailing ship, moving slower under wind power. Smoke swirls from the smokestack, covering the deck with soot and dirt. Sparks were also a danger.

△ **A passenger throws a disc** during a game on the deck of a steamer heading for Australia in the 1880s.

◁ **First-class passengers enjoy an afternoon party** on deck, sheltered from the sun by an awning of flags.

18

Up on deck, there was much more room for exercise. (The main deck of the *Great Eastern* was so wide and long that it was nicknamed 'Oxford Street'.) Here passengers strolled and sat. If they were lucky, they might catch sight of passing ships, whales, flying fish or even icebergs. There were plenty of deck games, including cricket, quoits and obstacle races. Some people brought guns on ship and shot at seabirds.

When the sea was calm, the bolder men jumped overboard for a swim. But they had to be cautious. They might be unable to catch up with the ship again, and it would steam on without them.

▽ **First-class passengers on the grand and ornate gallery of HMS *Calcutta***, painted by James Tissot.

IN THE ENGINE ROOM

One of the biggest treats for passengers was a tour of the engine room. It seemed like another world, with its choking heat, clanking pistons and hissing steam. But for those who kept the engines going, it was the hardest and worst job on board.

The stokers shovelled coal into the huge furnaces which heated water into steam. At first, the coal had to be brought in barrows from the stern. Later ships had fuel stores at the sides. Stokers worked for up to twelve hours at a time, shifting as much as 3 tonnes of coal. Others raked out the ashes and carried them away to be dumped overboard.

Engine rooms were very hot and airless. They often had no proper ventilation. Things were far worse in the scorching weather of the Red Sea or the Indian Ocean. Rough seas made the labour of lifting and shovelling even more difficult. But the stokers could never stop. The steam engines had to be kept going in all weathers.

▷ **A stoker feeds the ship's furnaces with coal** while an engineer checks the engines. Coal supplies were stored in holds at each side of the ship.

▷ **The sailing and engine crew** of the *Campania*. Built in 1893, it was then the world's largest ship. Extra coal was carried on board at one of the bunkering stations on its route. The coal was put on small boats that were towed out to the steamship and then unloaded using baskets.

▽ **The bridge of the steamship *Lucania*.** Orders altering the ship's speed were sent from the bridge house (out of view) down to the engine room.

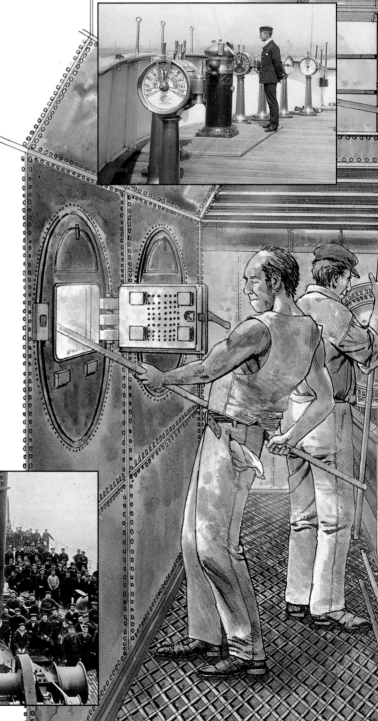

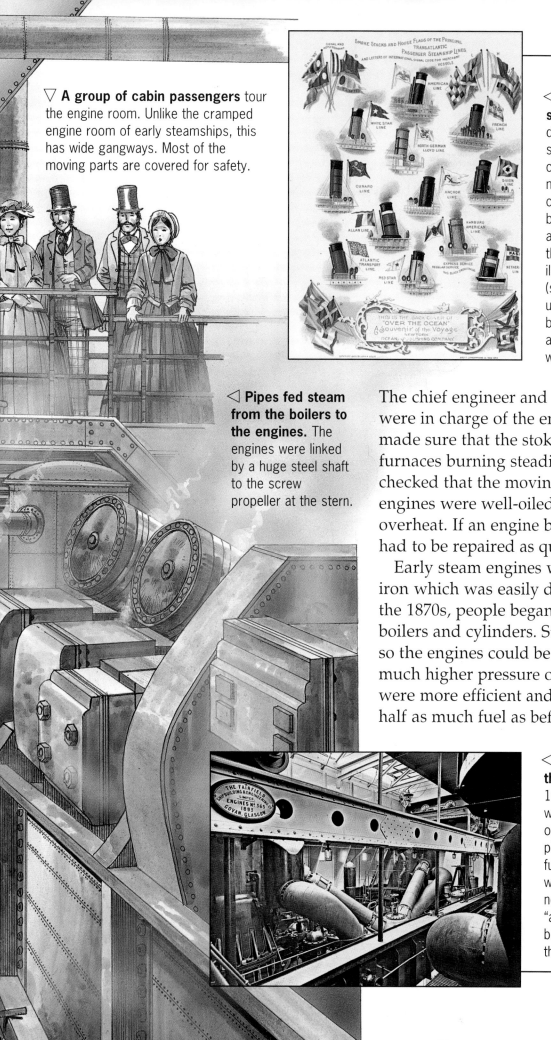

▽ **A group of cabin passengers** tour the engine room. Unlike the cramped engine room of early steamships, this has wide gangways. Most of the moving parts are covered for safety.

◁ **An 1893 steamship souvenir** showing the different designs for smoke stack (funnel) colours and flags of the major shipping companies on the routes between ports in Europe and New York. Shown at the top left of the illustration are pennants (small triangular flags) used to signal messages between steamships at sea before radios were invented.

◁ **Pipes fed steam from the boilers to the engines.** The engines were linked by a huge steel shaft to the screw propeller at the stern.

The chief engineer and his junior officers were in charge of the engines. They made sure that the stokers kept the furnaces burning steadily. They also checked that the moving parts of the engines were well-oiled and did not overheat. If an engine broke down, it had to be repaired as quickly as possible.

Early steam engines were made of cast iron which was easily damaged. Then in the 1870s, people began to use steel for boilers and cylinders. Steel was stronger, so the engines could be worked with a much higher pressure of steam. They were more efficient and burned less than half as much fuel as before.

◁ **The boiler room of the _Lucania_.** The date 1893, when the engines were built, can be seen on the left on a metal plaque on the joist. The funnels on the _Lucania_ were so big that a newspaper reported that "a mail coach could have been driven through them as if in a tunnel".

JOURNEY'S END

"Soon after ten o'clock, from the man aloft we heard 'Land'. Oh how all eyes were strained in the direction to which he pointed!" This is how an emigrant on a steamship describes his first sight of Australia in 1853.

As steamships became faster and more efficient, these massive voyages took less time. Passenger numbers also rose. Between the 1830s and 1901, 10 million emigrants left Britain by steamship to settle overseas. Over three-quarters of them went to the USA and Canada.

▽ **Steamship passengers from Britain arrive in New York in about 1850.**

GLOSSARY

bridge captain's control area on a ship's deck, usually with a 'house'.

bunkering station a place where ships could be refuelled with coal on long voyages.

clipper very fast sailing ship, with tall masts and sharp bow, which could 'clip' or shorten the times set by other vessels.

compass a device for finding direction. It has a magnetic needle which always points north.

cylinder the chamber in which an engine's piston moves.

emigrant a person leaving one country to live in another.

famine a disastrous shortage of food.

guinea old unit of money, worth one pound and one shilling (£1.05).

hull frame of a ship.

iron-clad wooden vessel covered in sheets of iron to protect it against cannon fire.

piston a solid engine part which fits inside a cylinder and is pushed back and forth by steam or another force.

port the left-hand side of a ship looking forwards.

quay a place where vessels are loaded or unloaded.

quoits a game in which iron or rope rings are thrown over a spike.

rigging the system of ropes, chains and tackle which holds up and controls sails and masts.

rudder a hinged plate at the stern of a ship which directs its course.

screw propeller a set of blades at the end of a shaft which, when turned, pushes the ship along.

starboard the right-hand side of a ship looking forwards.

steerage large living area below decks, usually above the rudder.

stern the back part of a ship (the front part is called the **bow**).

tugboat a small, powerful boat which pulls larger vessels.

▽ **Steamship routes from Britain.**
Journeys to the Far East became much quicker after the opening of the Suez Canal in Egypt in 1869. The canal linked the Mediterranean Sea with the Red Sea, cutting the distance to China (then part of the Manchu Empire) by ship by 48,000 kilometres and twelve days.

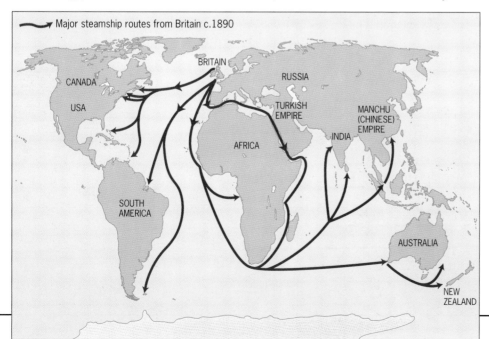

Major steamship routes from Britain c.1890

TIMECHART

1819 First steamship crosses the Atlantic (using sails as well).

1821 First iron ship, *Aaron Manby*, launched.

1836 First successful propeller made.

1837 Victoria becomes queen.

1838 *Great Western* makes first trip to USA.

1838 Samuel Cunard founds shipping line.

1840 Peninsular and Orient (P & O) shipping line founded.

1843 Launch of *Great Britain*, the first big iron ship.

1845 Potato famine in Ireland sparks emigration.

1849 Gold Rush to California.

1856 Improved steam engine built by John Elder.

1858 Launch of *Great Eastern*.

1863 First steel ship launched in Liverpool.

1869 Suez Canal opens.

1876 Plimsoll line introduced (this was a line on the ship's hull: if it was too near the water line, the ship was too heavily loaded. Many cargo ships had previously been lost through overloading).

1880s Use of sails on steamships abandoned.

1901 Death of Victoria.

23

INDEX